Massachusetts

Connecticut

Rhode Island

The Siege of Rhode Island

to Aiden Lincoln
love, Sassy

rember Onesimus + Moses 1776!
11.20

In memory of my maternal grandparents, Frances and Walter Wheeler Crane, for their unconditional love and support, and their mesmerizing stories about the life and adventures of John Crane.

*Linda Fitz Hooper*

www.mascotbooks.com

*General Crane: Hero of the American Revolution*

**For more information, please contact:**
Mascot Books
620 Herndon Parkway, Suite 320
Herndon, VA 20170
info@mascotbooks.com

Library of Congress Control Number: 2017915438

CPSIA Code: PRT1117A
ISBN-13: 978-1-68401-470-5

Printed in the United States

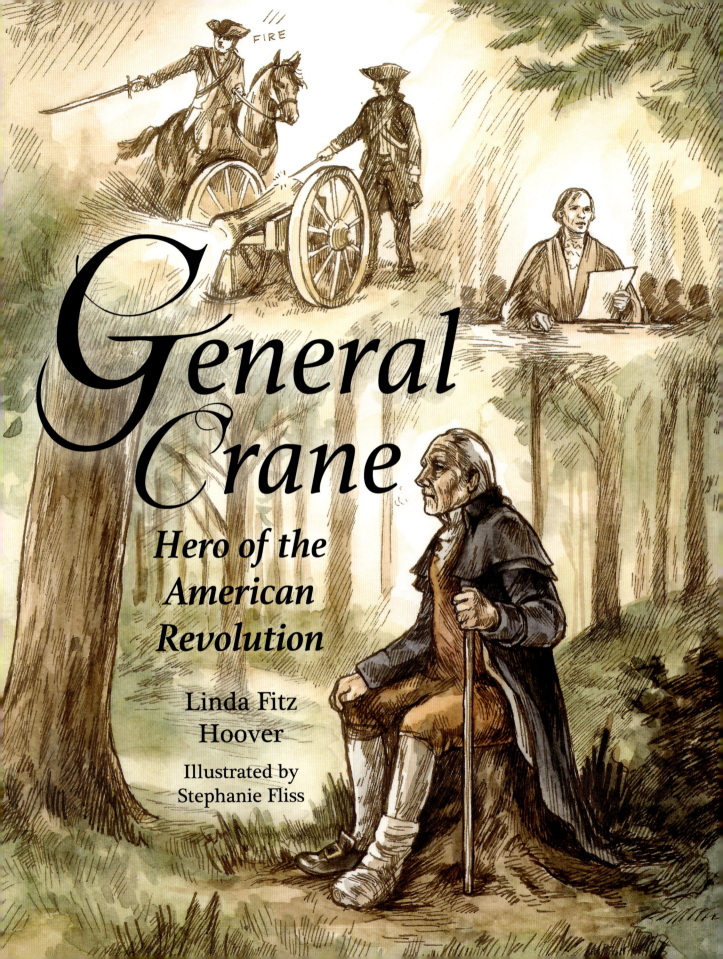

# General Crane

## Hero of the American Revolution

Linda Fitz
Hoover

Illustrated by
Stephanie Fliss

*J*ohn Crane was born on December 7, 1744 in Braintree, Massachusetts. John, his big brother Abijah, and his little sister Miriam helped their parents with chores and enjoyed singing songs, telling riddles, and playing with their friends.

John listened to stories about his great-grandfather Henry Crane, who came from England to Massachusetts in 1654. *What an exciting life Great-Grandfather had!* young John thought to himself. Little could he have imagined the adventures awaiting him in the years ahead!

In 1756, John's father, who was ill, was drafted to serve in the French and Indian War. John said, "Father, please stay here with our family. I will go in your place, and I will make the family proud." He was only 12 years old!

John Crane, will you be a brave soldier?

Yes, Sir. I will!

FACTS

The French and Indian War was from 1754 to 1763. Native Americans, including the Iroquois and Cherokee, assisted the British and British colonists, while members of Wabanaki, Algonquin, and Ojibwa assisted the French and French colonists. George Washington, who was 22 at the time, led the Virginia militia and helped the British to victory.

When John was 19, he and his brother moved to Boston and set up a shop. They became housewrights and helped build wooden homes in the growing city.

*J*ohn married Mehitable Wheeler when he was 22 years old.
They lived in a home on Tremont Street.

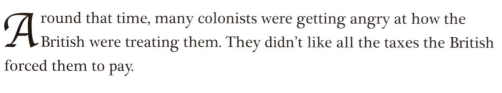

*A*round that time, many colonists were getting angry at how the British were treating them. They didn't like all the taxes the British forced them to pay.

In protest, some men in Boston organized a secret group called the Sons of Liberty. Its members included Samuel Adams, John Hancock, Paul Revere…and John Crane.

One afternoon, 17 Sons of Liberty met at John's shop to teach the British a lesson they would never forget. They decided to go down to the harbor, sneak aboard the British ships docked there, and throw crates of tea into the water. To disguise themselves, several painted their faces and dressed as Mohawk Indians.

As the Sons of Liberty headed toward the harbor, other men joined them. When they reached the ships, there were about 70 men in total who cheered from the docks as the Sons of Liberty threw tea overboard. The Boston Tea Party had begun!

*T*hen there was a terrible accident! One of the crates fell off the shelf onto John's head and knocked him out. Was he dead? The other Sons of Liberty dragged him to a nearby warehouse and hid him under the sawdust.

Then John woke up. He had a headache and a bump on his head, but he was fine!

John was the only patriot hurt in the Boston Tea Party. This was the first time, but not the last, that he would be injured for his country.

After the Boston Tea Party, things got worse for the people in Boston. John was worried. He wasn't getting enough carpentry work to take care of his family, so he and Mrs. Crane decided to leave Boston. They and their three young children—John, Alice, and Abijah—packed their things and moved to Providence, Rhode Island.

In Providence, John heard that the British had attacked colonists at Lexington and Concord and that the colonists were fighting at Bunker Hill. John said, "I am a soldier. I was trained in artillery when I lived in Boston. Now I must return!" He organized men from Rhode Island, and they marched to Roxbury, near Boston, to fight.

The Revolutionary War had begun!

After the battle, Gen. George Washington ordered his troops to march to New York—over 200 miles from Boston. Some officers like John rode horses, but his troops went by foot, taking care to safely move the cannons and other artillery on their journey.

O n the way to New York, whenever John saw a British ship or heard guns firing, he would get on his horse and head toward it. He was told again and again to not go out alone, but John always said, "The shot is not cast which is to kill me."

A British ship was causing trouble in the harbor of New York. Gen. Washington knew that John had excellent eyesight and artillery skills, so he asked him to be the one to fire on the ship. He did and chased the ship away, but later the ship returned and fired on John. John saw the cannon ball coming and leaned away from it, but it still hit him on the foot. John needed to get to a hospital fast!

*My dear brother,
deliver this money to
Mrs. Crane for her family.
Tell her he is doing well.
He is highly respected
in the Army and we
hope he can return soon.*

John was taken to a hospital in New Jersey. Back then, hospitals did not have the medicine or equipment that they do today, so John's foot became infected and he came down with lockjaw.

Col. Knox, the Commander of the Continental Artillery, was concerned about John and his family. He sent a letter to his brother with orders to visit Mrs. Crane and give her $50.

$J$ohn was strong and survived the infection. After he was treated, he returned home for Mrs. Crane to take care of him.

The Army told John to stay home because of his injuries. They wanted to pay him a pension as well, but John refused it, telling them the soldiers needed the money more than he did. He stamped his injured foot and said, "No Sir, they never shall say that I eat their bread when I have done serving them."

$T$hat spring when he was better, John returned to the battlefield. He
was promoted to Colonel and given the Third Continental Artillery to
command. The soldiers were very glad that he was back.

M any soldiers weren't getting the money they were owed, so they couldn't afford shoes, warm clothes, or good food. John and other officers complained to Gen. Washington, who was such a caring leader he personally went to Philadelphia to tell the Continental Congress to help the soldiers.

It was very cold when John's Third Continental Artillery marched to Valley Forge in Pennsylvania. There was rain and snow, and the soldiers were freezing and hungry. They built log huts to live in through the winter. That spring, more food and clothing arrived. Gen. Washington's troops were ready to fight!

New York

Pennsylvania

The Battle of Springfield

New Jersey

The Battle of Monmouth

Maryland

Delaware

Massachusetts

Connecticut

Rhode Island

The Siege of Rhode Island

For the next six years, Col. Crane's cannons roared.

In 1783, Gen. Washington promoted Col. Knox to be the nation's first Secretary of War, leaving open the position of Commander of the Continental Artillery.

There was only one man for the job in Gen. Washington's mind. He asked John if he would take Col. Knox's place as Commander. John snapped his heels together and saluted sharply. "YES, SIR!"

John was promoted to Brigadier General, but after a couple of months, Gen. Crane resigned. We're not sure why, but we do know that he, Gen. Knox, and other officers were still very angry at how their soldiers were being treated. One theory is that he resigned in protest.

In 1783, after eight years of fighting to gain our independence. John returned home for good to his family, which had grown to include six children. He didn't want his countrymen to forget about the Revolutionary War, so he was among the first to join The Society of the Cincinnati, which is comprised of officers who had fought in the War.

One day, John got a message from John Hancock, who was now the Governor of Massachusetts. They had both been members of the Sons of Liberty many years ago, and John was eager to see his old friend again.

Gov. Hancock told John that to thank him for his service, he wanted to deed him land in the northern District of Maine, near the port city of Machias. And he had another offer, if John was interested. You see, Maine needed a Judge of Common Pleas, and Gov. Hancock could only think of one man honest and fair enough to take the job: John Crane!

Naturally, John agreed.

For the next 13 years, John tended to his lumber business. He also traveled up and down the coast of Maine, holding court in the small towns that were springing up as settlements grew. Sometimes, when he was near what is now the town of Thomaston, he would stop and visit his old commander, Henry Knox.

John's children grew up and married, and by 1804 he and Mrs. Crane had more than a dozen grandchildren. They loved to gather around their grandfather and listen to stories of his past.

Then one day John hurt his foot again. He could no longer conduct business or travel by horse to hold court. How would he take care of Mrs. Crane? He was a proud man and always said he would never take a military pension, but now he had no choice. Twenty years after he left the Army, John filled out the paperwork to make sure his wife would always be cared for.

John went outside and sat under the Maine pines. He thought back on everything he had done in life.

*A patriot who served in the French and Indian War when he was 12.*

*One of the Sons of Liberty, and the only one injured at the Boston Tea Party.*

*One of the first Rhode Islanders to heed the calls for Independence after the Battles of Lexington and Concord.*

*Commander of the Continental Artillery.*

*Maine's Judge of Common Pleas for 13 years.*

How could that young John of Braintree possibly have imagined the adventures that he had lived? John Crane, American Hero indeed!

To learn more about John Crane
and the Third Continental Artillery:

★ Enjoy a reenactment of Crane's Artillery of Newport in Rhode Island.

★ Tour the many historical sites in Boston and throughout Massachusetts.

★ Visit the monument honoring John Crane in Whiting, Maine.

★ Learn about Valley Forge at the Valley Forge National Park in Pennsylvania.

★ See other Revolutionary War sites where Crane's Third Artillery fought.

## About the Author:

Linda Fitz Hoover grew up in an Air Force family and lived on three continents as a child. She holds advanced degrees in psychology and public administration, and has worked in educational, social service, and healthcare settings. Her hobbies include amateur astronomy, birding, reading, and genealogy. She and her husband Dennis have one grown son, Brian, who lives in Washington, DC. They live in Pensacola, Florida.

Linda is active in the Daughters of the American Revolution, Pensacola Chapter. Her DAR patriot is her sixth great-grandfather, John Crane.

## Have a book idea?
### Contact us at:

info@mascotbooks.com | www.mascotbooks.com

New York

The Battle of Springfield

Pennsylvania

New Jersey

The Battle of Monmouth

Maryland

Delaw